This book is dedicated to Sarah, who daily fills my life with joy.

Edited by Aileen Andres Sox
Designed by Dennis Ferree
Art by Mary Rumford
Typeset in 14/18 Weiss

ISBN: 0-8163-1125-0

98 99 00 01 02 • 5 4 3 2

Happy Birthday Tomorrow to Me!

By Linda Porter Carlyle   Illustrated by Mary Rumford

Pacific Press® Publishing Association
Nampa, Idaho
Oshawa, Ontario, Canada

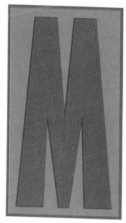

ama, can I come get in your bed?"

"Come on," answers Mama's sleepy voice.

I hurry down the hallway. It is very cold. Mama holds the covers up, and I crawl in. I crawl right on over her. I like to be in the middle.

Hold still," says Mama softly. "What time is it?" Her eyes are shut.

I can see the red numbers on the clock beside the bed. They shine in the darkness. "It's 6-1-5," I whisper.

"Don't wiggle," Mama says, "I'm not ready to wake up."

 lie quietly. Here we are, all in a cozy row. Mama and me and Papa and Joshua. I lie quietly and listen. Mama breathes softly and slowly. Papa makes little sputtery sounds. Joshua is purring.

"Mama!" I whisper.

"Sh-h-h," she says. "I'm asleep."

retty soon the clock beside the bed will buzz. Papa will groan and reach out his arm from under the covers and turn it off.

"Stop squirming," Mama mumbles.

"Mama! Tomorrow's my birthday! It's almost here!"

ama gives me a squeeze. "Happy birthday tomorrow," she says. Her eyes are shut, but her mouth is smiling.

"Happy birthday tomorrow to you," says Papa. He rolls over on his back and stretches.

I giggle and wiggle. "Happy birthday tomorrow to me!"

oday is a long, long day. I can't sit still. I am waiting for tomorrow. Tomorrow I will be bigger and older. "Go outside," says Mama. "Go outside and swing."

I swing as high as I can go. I swing mightily.

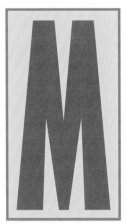ama comes out the back door carrying the picnic quilt. Oh, boy! We will have lunch on the lawn. I help Mama smooth the blanket on the grass.

"Tomorrow's my birthday!" I say, with a mouthful of sandwich.

"Yes, I believe I heard that somewhere," Mama answers. Her eyes twinkle at me. "Do you know the name of what you are feeling?" she asks. "It's joy."

fall backward and stretch my arms and legs out straight. I
see the clouds floating overhead. I like the feeling of joy.